Knowing, understanding and living with your dog

Second Edition

VAL BONNEY

First published 1996
by Bonnie's Dog Obedience and Care Centre
34 Romea Street
The Gap, Queensland, Australia

© Bonnie's Dog Obedience and Care Centre 1996

Printed in Australia by
Watson Ferguson & Company, Brisbane
Reprinted 1996
Extended Edition 1997
Reprinted 1998
Second Edition 1999
Reprinted 2001

National Library of Australia
Cataloguing-in-Publication data

Bonney, Val, 1936–.
Who's the boss? : knowing, understanding
and living with your dog.

2nd ed.
ISBN 0 646 38155 5
1. Dogs - Training. I. Bonnie's Dog Obedience and
Care Centre. II Title.

636.70887

All rights reserved. Apart from any fair dealing for the
purposes of private study, research, criticism or review,
as permitted under the Copyright Act, no part may be
reproduced by any process without written permission.
Enquiries should be made to the publisher.

Editing and management by
Janette Whelan Publishing Consultancy

Design and makeup by
Ads-Up Graphics Pty Ltd

Illustrations by Brenda Biggs,
a lover of dogs, especially
the bearded collie

$\mathcal{D}$edicated to

all those who have given their time and energy in trying to understand the dog a little better, and who have passed on their knowledge through books, courses, lectures and seminars, and to those who have worked tirelessly in dog obedience clubs, giving their time freely and for no personal acknowledgement

the late Roger Hayden, who devoted more than twenty years to the dog squad of Corrective Services, and encouraged me to write this book

a German shepherd named King, who first taught me so much about dog behaviour and the joy of owning a dog

Why should I read this book?

- I want my dog to live with me without creating problems.
- I want my children and my dog to play together safely.
- I want my dog to fit in with my family.
- I want the greatest understanding and companionship from my pet.
- I want to know more about pack structure and how important it is in the raising of a puppy.
- I want to bond with my dog and have a loyal companion for many years.
- I want to understand more about the dog, which will help me with better obedience control.
- I want to know what is necessary in order to be a responsible pet owner.

$\mathcal{C}$ontents

$\mathcal{P}$reface

This book is for people who may or may not know anything about dogs, but who want to find the key to open the door to a happy home with their obedient dog.

Over the last thirty or forty years, many who have studied dog behaviour and many who have trained dogs and their handlers have written some wonderful books on dogs. From their knowledge and those who have provided courses on dog training and behaviour, we have gained much. This has allowed dog trainers, dog obedience clubs and the public to enter the dog training world with a solid foundation and a chance at success.

However, there must be something missing. Why?

Because the dog problems continue and the public and governments are not sure how to go about correcting them.

This book can go part of the way to eradicating many problems if the section on pack structure is taken to heart and applied properly to the dog and the family situation.

Read it, think about it, discuss it, and apply the lessons lovingly and carefully to your pet:

- It works.
- It will prevent many problems from occurring.

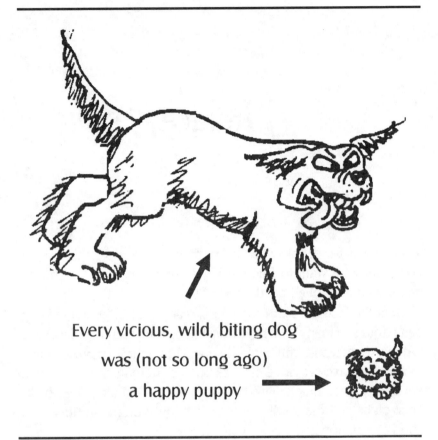

Every vicious, wild, biting dog
was (not so long ago)
a happy puppy

- If a problem has already occurred it can be put right very quickly if the pack structure is put in order.

Understanding must precede training.

Pack structure Understanding and application	+	**Early puppy training** from 8 weeks of age	=	**Missing link**

The missing link is, therefore, the understanding and application of pack structure *plus* early puppy training.

Over my many years of training dogs and advising owners how to handle their dogs, I have met some wonderful and caring people. I think that more people now care about their dog and are prepared to spend some valuable time out of their busy lives learning about and training their pet.

I have been conducting puppy classes for the last twelve years and have seen the results of mature and steady dogs, problem-free, in happy homes.

Right now, to my delight, puppy training is taking off in leaps and bounds. An environment free of dog problems will, we hope, be the result.

Puppy training has taken off because the enormous benefits that come from early puppy socialisation and guided instruction on the importance of puppy play schools have been recognised as essential and basic to the dog's adult behaviour and maturity. Early training prevents future problems.

I wouldn't be surprised if puppy training from eight weeks of age became a must in every shire, city, county, state and territory in the not-too-distant future.

Breeders who are forward-thinking will advise buyers to attend puppy management sessions conducted by knowledgeable people. Puppy trainers must know and understand the full importance of pack structure and how to apply it in the raising of a puppy and the owning of a dog.

A puppy properly raised will become a sound, confident and mature dog.

This book will take you through:
- alpha pack structure
- understanding body language of the dog
- some behavioural problems
- puppy management.

In every situation, keep asking yourself 'Who's the boss?' If you keep getting the answer 'I am!', then you will know that you are winning.

Good reading, and may you share many joys with your canine companion.

Val Bonney

$\mathcal{W}$ hat makes a dog tick?

Why does a dog do the things it does?

It is very important always to keep in mind that this lovely little bundle of fur that you have just adopted into your family derives its origins from the wolf.

It is, and always will be, a canine and, as such, it has all the natural heritage and instincts that a wolf has. It doesn't matter how small or big your dog is. A dog has thousands of years of heritage and instinct, and yet we take this wild creature and ask it to live in a domestic situation where everything is foreign to it.

There is *nothing human* about your new friend. It will be a little like owning your own private 'ET'. Although your pet is not an extra-terrestrial visitor from outer space, it is, however, a different species from you. Remember, it is not and never will be human, and so you cannot expect it to act like you. Your pup won't think like you, talk like you, eat like you or walk like you. So it is very important you understand something of your dog's psychology and physiology.

When we take a dog from a litter of beautiful little puppies and bring it into our home, we tend to expect that there is nothing for this little creature to learn. We think the pup will automatically fit into our home and be one of the family without any effort from us. But the pup which understands from birth its place in the domestic environment *does not exist.*

Remember, this bundle of fur (with its natural instincts) is not used to living in a house environment. It must be taught how to do this, and the teacher is *you.*

A dog's sight, hearing, and sense of smell are very different from ours. We, as responsible pet owners, should take a little time to think about these senses so that we can appreciate the importance of the part they play in our dog's lifestyle. We need to understand them better. If we understand them, obedience and having a happy mate will be easy to achieve.

Sight

A dog's sight is not quite as good as yours with stationary objects, but when movement occurs, the dog sees it with remarkable speed and all its attention will be focused on the moving object (since the dog is a natural predator).

Your pet's peripheral vision is wider than yours, because, in most breeds, the eyes are situated slightly off-centre, rather than directly in front. The peripheral vision allows the dog to see wider and higher than we can. This is why we sometimes think the dog has eyes in the back of its head, especially if it has just done something wrong. 'How did my pet see me coming?' It only has to catch movement from you, no matter how small, to know you are there.

Dogs don't judge distance as well as humans do, but can detect movement over a much wider field of vision. No wonder it is so hard to catch the little rascal in the act of being destructive and be able to reprimand it.

Eyesight — a stationary ball is not
easily seen by a dog.

Hearing

A dog's hearing is also different from ours. We go to school and learn to read and write. Verbal communication (speech) is very important to us. We learn to spell the words we hear, and look at pictures of them on the blackboard.

Repetition and confirmation over many years give us the confidence to act out the words we use and understand what we are doing. A dog does not have these advantages. It has never been to school, and does not understand the English language. However,

3

the dog *does* understand tones and sounds. With its sharp interpretation of body language, it quickly puts two and two together.

Your dog's hearing formulates itself as an *echo*. Have you ever stood on top of a mountain and called out 'Hello'? You get nothing back. But if you call out Helloo-oo,what you hear in return is the LOOOO. Although I am not aware of any documented evidence of this hearing phenomenom, I believe, after many years of observation, that the dog does hear the echoes which words make.

Understanding this hearing aspect of your dog will make the very early training and teaching of your dog so much easier.

HELLO-O-O-O

—O-O-O-O-O—

Hearing — dogs are very much
sound-oriented creatures.

Drag out the training words you use, for example, 'Siiit', 'Dooown', 'Staaand', 'Cooome'. Sounds silly to you possibly, but it is understood faster and more easily by the dog. The vowel is where the emphasis should be.

The dog's hearing capacity is about seven times greater than ours, so it should never be necessary for you to shout at your best friend. (I wonder how many of us can put this into practice!) It's not always easy to remember this hearing aspect of our companion, but it is very important.

Remember, your dog can hear high notes in ultrasonic ranges which humans cannot. With low notes, limits are similar for dogs and humans. As frequencies rise, the dog's ears become more sensitive than ours.

Smell

Your dog's nose is its communication antenna. It is one of the most important senses your dog has. By using this sense, your dog distinguishes between friend and foe, where it has been and where it is going.

It has been estimated that a dog's sense of smell is at least 100,000 times greater than ours. Many experts will rate it even higher. It is a very powerful organ which your pet has at its disposal.

A dog's sense of smell is so great that it can trace lost people, find a track through rough and frozen terrain, find particular articles such as drugs, or smell a bitch on heat many kilometres away. Dogs have been known to walk thousands of kilometres across countries to return to their homes. (How do they do this? Have they other senses and skills we don't know about?)

The very ground your pet walks on must be like a smorgasbord.

5

Smell — a dog's sense of smell is at least 100,000 times better than a human's.

The number of different fragrances which your dog can smell is incredible.

When a dog sniffs at a strange dog, it is the initial investigation into finding out all about this new canine. Other features like posture and eye contact (staring) play an important part also, but if they each like what they find, they could start playing. However, if they don't like what they have discovered about each other, your chances of having a dog fight are fairly high.

From a handler's point of view, sniffing at other dogs is to be discouraged. Remember, if you are out walking your dog, don't let it sniff at a strange dog. Keep your dog walking. Don't stop.

Communication – dogs learning
about each other.

I.Q. – the ability to reason

A dog's ability to reason has been researched by many prominent people, and it has been found not to be as high as we would imagine. Intelligence is hard to measure, and several factors need to be taken into consideration:

- breed
- size of dog
- amount of training
- ancestry
- upbringing
- temperament.

I.Q. level — a dog's lack of reasoning power means that it is susceptible to conditioning.

However, to my knowledge, a dog's reasoning power compares with that of an eighteen-month to two-year-old child. Amazing, isn't it?

The huge advantage the dog has is its thousands of years of heritage and instinct mentioned earlier. This gives your pet attributes and abilities that we, as human beings, do not understand. I believe that we are able to use effectively about 15 per cent of our dog's brain capacity.

There is still so much for us to learn. This new friend of yours is, remember, a totally separate species. It is not human. *Don't ever forget this.*

Remembering these things will help you to understand and live with this wonderful creature we call a dog.

Other senses

Dogs have an inbuilt sense of direction and time, and lose only about one minute in every twenty-four hours. If, for example, you feed your dog each day at 5 p.m., then it will be waiting for you to feed it again at 5 p.m., one minute to 5 p.m., or one minute past 5 p.m. the next day. The same thing applies to taking your dog for a walk, or any other daily habit in your family. These become established patterns and could create problems.

Think what this means to your dog's behaviour patterns and your training techniques. We all think we have control of our dog, but think about it honestly, 'Who trains whom in your home?'

$\mathcal{P}$ack structure

The ladder of life

If the only thing you learn to understand and use effectively is the *pack structure* (pecking order) around which the dog's whole lifestyle revolves, then you will have one of the best-behaved, happy, easy-to-live with dogs it is possible to have.

This doesn't just happen. You have to be aware of what is required to make it all happen.

An old but very valid expression used by many is: 'A super dog is made not born.'

What is this thing called 'pack structure'?

A dog is born, lives its whole life and dies within a thing called 'pack structure'. Don't try to get your dog to live outside it because you will fail.

The pack structure is the dog's whole way of life. It is how it lives within a community of other canines or with your family. If you do not understand this pack structure you will never be quite sure how or when to correct it. The result will be doubt and confusion for the dog and frustration for you.

If you want to train your dog, you must be the 'pack leader' — the 'alpha dog'. Then you will have peace and understanding in your home.

Dogs are very social creatures. They have their hierarchy, but they are never equal in rank.

It might be easier for you to understand this very important pack structure if I liken it to a ladder. In the wild, if ten dogs run together as a pack, only one dog is the boss (the alpha dog). This alpha dog is in total control of its pack. Every other dog which lives within the boundaries of this pack answers to the leader. It is usually the strongest and most dominant member and it sits on the *top rung* of the ladder.

Every other member of this pack of ten dogs is placed on rungs going down the ladder. They place themselves in order of dominance, with the most submissive dog on the bottom rung. Remember that no two dogs can be equal, and so no two dogs will be side by side on any one rung.

To change its place on this ladder (in the pack structure), a dog has to push the dog above it, until it forces that dog to change places with it. They challenge each other.

For example, let's call two dogs Peter and Paul. Peter is above Paul on the ladder of life. Paul has to pay his due respects to Peter if he is to survive within this pack. However, as time passes, Paul decides he is a larger and stronger dog than Peter. It is now time for Paul to challenge Peter for his position.

To do this, Paul has to prove his dominance over Peter, and this means that these two dogs will possibly have a fight. How nasty this fight becomes depends on just how much Paul really wants Peter's position, and how much Peter wants to hold it. If Paul wins,

The challenge — climbing the ladder of life
in the pack structure.

he now moves up into the position previously held by Peter, and Peter moves down a rung into the position which was held by Paul.

Of course, they don't always fight. Sometimes a strong stare or dominant body posture will be enough to turn the tide. However, the pack will know something has happened, even if we humans don't. Those of you who own several dogs should keep your eyes open and watch for any change in the pack structure. When there has been a change, you must accept this change and put the new top dog in the pack *first*. This takes some discipline on your part, as you may have been giving first place to a faithful old friend for many years.

Understanding this code of behaviour by which a dog lives will make it possible for us to correct and control our dogs without causing undue stress.

If we do not take the time to learn about this pack structure, we are doing ourselves and the dog a great disservice. This lack of knowledge is the reason for most of the problems we have with our dogs, particularly in the home environment.

You can love your dog to death, but if it has no respect for you as its alpha leader, you have nothing of any worth to give it. Your dog will *not* understand you or respect you, and confusion, barking and snarling will reign. Your once-lovely puppy is now confused.

We take a puppy out of its natural environment where it is living within a pack of its sisters and brothers, which is the environment the puppy totally understands and loves. We take it home with us to live in a domestic situation with (to the puppy) funny-looking animals which, for a start, walk on two legs, and not four. Poor puppy, it must be so confused.

Children on the ladder

To the dog's way of thinking, young children are always below it in the pack structure (remember, to the dog, children are also animals). This is because the young do not have the confidence and maturity required by the dog for it to accept their control.

This little pup which, in its fifth, sixth and seventh weeks of life is just learning to live and know its place in the litter, now has to readjust its whole way of life. These humans it is now required to live with expect different things from it. No longer can it, for instance, do the natural thing of going to the toilet whenever and wherever it wishes. So the pack leader has to show it what to do and teach it where to go.

Even a dog living in a domestic situation, like its wild brother or sister, needs a pack leader, and that leader has to be *you*, the owner. Remembering the ladder and the rungs of that ladder, your family members will be placed on the rungs in the order in which the *dog* sees them.

Looking at all of this from the dog's point of view (it is now necessary for you to try to *think* like a dog!), the dog must find it not only difficult but also almost impossible in some situations and families to see a child under the age of 10 or 12 years as being above it in the pack structure. This is one reason so many young children get bitten. Other reasons, of course, could be children's behavioural patterns and their unpredictability.

In a family of, say, two adults and three children, with the children ranging in age from 10 years to 3 months, the pecking order (to the dog's way of thinking) will be, in the majority of cases, father, mother, *dog*, then the children.

If the parents understand this about their dog, the family of six will live together very amicably. The parents will understand that any play between the pup and the children must be supervised.

If, however, this pecking order is not understood, trouble in the form of biting, growling, and so on can, and probably will, eventuate.

Young children do not have the power to be in control of their pet. Dogs will look after the young, will play with the children,

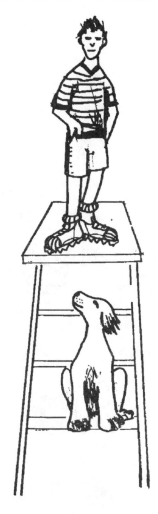

Pack structure is out of order.

Pack structure is in correct order.

Who's the boss here?

A family of father, mother and three very young children. Note the dog's place from the dog's point of view. This is in order.

safeguard them, and love them. But they will not, generally, take orders from them. They may see an order or a face-to-face encounter from a child as a challenge, and retaliate.

Many children get bitten by dogs every year, especially on or near the face. These bites could be avoided if parents (and the trainers who advise them) understand and take seriously the dog's pack structure and what it means to the dog in its daily life.

Whenever a child and a dog come face to face, even for a few seconds, the chances of a bite to the face are very real. Another cause of bites to the face is when the dog has been excited by running around the yard playing with the children and the dog jumps up to say to the child 'Come and play with me'. The dog does not want the play to stop.

Challenges to other dogs in the wild over food, territory or position of authority occur almost daily. We must realise that these challenges are a big part of the dog's thousands of years of heritage. Young children are no match for this powerful instinct.

The dog is not being aggressive, *it is simply being a dog.*

In this situation, adults should separate the pup from the area and supervise all future play with the pup until the children are old enough to understand that this real-life creature is not a toy.

In a pack of wild dogs, it is the older, stronger and often larger dog which is higher on the rungs of the ladder. The young child is seen as being weaker and less dominant and therefore, in the dog's mind, is below it in authority — at least one rung down — and that is where it will stay until the child is more mentally and emotionally mature.

Therefore, trouble will be caused by parents who do not, or will not, try to understand the way their pet thinks.

Let's look at an example. If the dog and a 3-year-old child both run to greet dad when he comes home from work, the dog will often push between the father and the child. If this happens, and the father pushes the dog away and picks up the child first, the father (in the dog's mind) is elevating the child above the dog in the pack structure. *This will not be acceptable to the dog. It will be confused and may retaliate.*

WRONG — father pushes the dog away, thus elevating the young child over the dog in the pack structure. Problems will arise if the dog is of a dominant nature.

Usually, the dog which has been pushed away will, after a short time, retaliate by biting or growling at the child. A problem has now been created. Dad and mum get angry and the dog gets into trouble for being aggressive. Possibly mum and dad may even decide to find another home for this particular dog. But problems will not occur if the pack structure, as described earlier, is not tipped off balance.

So what is the solution? All the dog needed in this case was a quick pat and recognition by the father. Then dad can pay as much attention as he wishes to the child. Dogs are *instant* creatures, and that quick pat is all that is required to satisfy its natural instincts.

Remember and understand that dogs do not think like us. They are not human — I cannot emphasise this too much. Don't try to turn your pooch into a carbon copy of yourself. Understand your pet's needs, and you will continue to have a joy to own.

You — the owner — must always be the alpha in the pack.

The dog will periodically challenge even you for the top-dog role. Expect this to occur, particularly throughout the early years of the dog's life, but don't ever allow it to win any challenge it may offer. Don't be cruel — be firm. Be sure the dog recognises you as the boss. Then go on with what you were doing.

Challenges to your authority will be given in many small ways. Watch for them, and know what is happening. The dog may growl at you. *Do not allow it.* Correct it immediately (the method of doing this will be discussed in chapter 4 under 'Reprimands'). If your pup or dog growls at you and you don't have the full confidence to correct and stop it, you need to contact an understanding trainer to help you overcome this initial dominance. Do not put it off or use force.

Your pet may suddenly not hear what you are telling it to do. It is deliberately testing you. Are you in control or not? That is what your dog is trying to find out. *Never allow disobedience to go*

RIGHT — father greets the dog first, then the child. In the dog's mind, it is above the child in the pack structure and should be greeted first.

uncorrected. If you do, you have shown yourself as a weak and inconsistent master/leader. These are only a couple of areas in which your dog can challenge you. There are many ways: pulling at pants, mouthing your hands or legs, developing selective hearing, refusing to obey a command you have given.

It is important that after every form of correction or discipline you follow it up immediately with praise. To do this, get your dog to 'sit' for you, and as soon as it does so, praise it.

So who *is* the boss? *You* decide. If it's to be you, then you *must* take it to heart yourself and teach your family members all about pack structure. If you do this, any problems you may encounter will be very small and easily corrected.

Obedience trainers and instructors who notice that a particular person is constantly having trouble getting the dog to pay attention should question the person to ascertain if the pack structure is in place.

Who's the boss here? Behavioural problems arise when the pack structure is out of kilter.

Pack structure is the most important part of understanding your pet and must be in place in order to achieve obedience. Get this right, and teaching, training and generally living with your pet will be a breeze.

As I have already said, you can love your pet to death, but if it has no respect for you as the alpha (leader) of the pack, there will be confusion, and living with your dog will not be pleasant. The dog has to learn to live with you, not the other way around. A dog is the best friend and companion you can have, provided all is in order and the dog's 'ladder of life' stays upright.

Best friends!

$\mathcal{B}$ody language

Learn to read your dog's body language from the moment it comes to live with you.

Unlike people, who use verbal communication extensively, the dog has to rely on *body language* as its main source of communication not only with other dogs but also with us.

Watch two or more pups at play. This is the best way of learning about your pet's methods of body communication. They talk to each other all the time. Tails may wag when greeting another dog or human, especially if they like what they scent and see. Hackles (hair along the dog's back) may rise and stand on end if they don't like what or who they scent and see.

Two dogs meeting for the first time will use their noses (scent) and will sniff at both ends of the dog they are meeting. If they wish to play because they like what they have found in each other, they will go into what we call a play bow. Front legs go down and the rear end rises. Ears normally prick (if they have ears that can stand up straight), and they will dance around each other. They will lunge at each other and emit sounds that, to the uninitiated, can sound like growls. They are possibly laughing with and at each other.

Play bow — 'Let's have some fun!'

However, if they don't like what they find, a brawl can eventuate. They may growl and show teeth, their ears may stand up straight, and their lips will curl back. Don't try to interfere if a fight develops. You could get bitten.

It is a good policy when you are walking your family pet to get into the habit of *never* allowing your dog to sniff at any strange dogs which may approach it. It doesn't need this type of socialisation.

I am presuming you are a good and responsible owner, and that you are walking with your dog *on a lead*. Should a strange dog on the prowl approach your dog, my advice is to tell your dog 'Leave' and keep your dog walking. Do not allow it to stop and make communication by sniffing. The most important thing is *keep walking*.

If you never allow your dog to sniff at a strange dog while you are out, your chances of having a dog fight develop will be cut by about 95 per cent. It will make walking your pooch so much more

24

pleasant. This comes under maintaining control of your dog. Remember, you are not responsible for anyone else's dog, but you should have total control over your own.

Marking territory

Dogs may want to lift their legs and urinate all over the place when walking. They can urinate dozens of times over a short distance.

Marking territory.

Don't let them do this. Tell them 'No' and keep walking, taking them with you. All they are doing with this constant urination is marking territory.

Marking territory is the leaving of their scent over another dog's scent to dominate the position. Dominate, dominate, dominate — this is the pack structure and is a powerful instinct in the dog's life.

The footpaths and areas in which you walk are *not* your dog's territory, so why should you allow the dog to mark them? The only territory your dog owns is its own yard.

A dog has a need to go to the toilet a couple of times daily. *Don't let it become territorial.* Dogs can and often will fight over territory they believe they own. Accept that this is part of being a dog, and don't allow your dog to mark what is really not its to mark.

If you don't allow your dog to mark just outside your gate for instance, your dog may then consider the fence as its boundary and it won't want to go outside of or over this boundary (fence).

Bitches are not normally as territorial as the dog. However, as in most things, there can be the exception. If you have a bitch who is showing signs of being extremely territorial, then treat her in the same manner you would a dog.

Paying attention

When using your dog's name, get your dog to look at you. Use your body language to do this, and watch your dog respond with its body language.

The dog who looks at the person talking to it is showing respect and submission. It is also much more pleasant to have a dog look at you when you speak to it. At least then you can see whether or not it is understanding and *paying attention* to what you are telling it to do. Right from the time it is a puppy, you should teach your dog to look at you. Hold it gently by both sides of the head and

Companionship — the joy of owning a pooch.

look into its eyes (but only for a few seconds at a time). If it stays quiet and looks at you, then it accepts you as the boss and you have achieved the desired result. (Don't forget to praise it!) If it squirms and doesn't want to look at you at all, then guess who is in charge?

It should sit in front of you, look up, prick its ears (even dogs with floppy ears can raise them a fraction), and move its head a little to let you know it is listening to what you are saying. It will also look extremely happy. After all, you're talking to it, aren't you?

If you show an interest in this faithful friend of yours, it will pay attention and want to be with you all the time. If your dog looks at you when you speak to it, then you are winning and it will be much easier for you to give it a command. This is what we are trying to achieve.

Pawing

When a dog starts pawing at you, it is seeking your attention. It is making demands on you. It will do this to another dog to gain its attention. Watch an older dog very firmly ignore this from a young pup if it does not want to play. You should do the same.

Don't allow your dog to make demands. In its own way it is being dominant if it continues with this action after you have ignored it. Of course, there may be times when you enjoy this. You may regard it as showing affection. Remember, if you allow your dog to jump up on you when playing, it will do the same thing to children. The dog's paws and claws on children can be disastrous.

Licking

Understand why the dog likes to lick, but once again it is not necessary that you allow it. A dog, being the social creature it is, likes to lick as a form of greeting. In the wild, however, it can have a meaning other than greeting. When the older dogs leave the pack to go hunting for food, they leave behind the juvenile members. On returning from the hunt, the pups will greet the returning oldies (male and female) by licking their mouths, saying 'Hello, I'm glad to see you', but more significantly asking them to regurgitate some of the food they have just hunted. This is done by licking from the

Pawing for attention — making a demand on the owner. Don't give in until you are ready. Demands can become challenges.

centre of the mouth towards the corners. The pup then gets fed. Isn't nature wonderful?

Dogs do not need to have this regurgitation of food from us, because we will feed them adequately anyway, but the instinct is still within this domesticated pet we have. Perhaps understanding this little process will help you not to get annoyed the next time

Licking at the mouth — this is a form of
greeting, but also stems from heritage and
instinct as a demand to be fed.

your pet wants to lick your mouth. If you don't want this to happen
to you, keep your face far enough away so that your dog can't reach
it.

Body language between
the older dog and the new pup

When a new pup is introduced into the house, we tend to expect
the older dog to accept this interloper without any sign of upset or
even aggression. We really do ask a lot of our old friend. If we

understand the pack structure, then it can be done without too many hassles. If, however, we still don't understand the pecking order, we are in for a few unpleasant surprises.

When bringing home the new puppy, it is a good idea to have someone take the older dog for a walk for a few hours. Bring the new addition to the family home and install it in the house before the older dog (first dog) is bought back home. Spread the scent of the new puppy around the house and around the yard as well. Walk the puppy into every room and along every verandah and patio where the older dog is allowed to go. Walk the puppy around every part of the yard and under the house that the older dog frequents.

The new pup is now established within the home territory. This will make it easier for the older dog to accept this interloper into the pack order.

Then it's time to introduce the older dog to the new puppy. Allow the older dog to see the new puppy walking around the house or yard and to go up to the new puppy and sniff it. Keep this first meeting under your close supervision. Don't forget that the older dog is the senior dog in the pack, so don't push it out of the way. The pup and the older dog will very soon be the best of friends. As a matter of fact, the pup will soon be driving the older dog crazy with its youthful exuberance. If you watch closely over the next six to twelve months you will see how much patience an older dog has with the puppy. They very often have far more patience than we have. Respect your older dog for this.

The pup will make overtures to the older dog, and usually the older dog will respond either by ignoring the pup totally or by getting up and moving away, or growling slightly at it. If this happens, the pup will get the message loud and clear and remove itself for a short time.

Remember, dogs understand each other's body language, and as the human owner we can only cause problems if we interfere.

31

The patience of an older dog with a puppy —
far more patience than humans have! Watch
and learn from your older dog.

Leave them to adjust and they will very quickly come to terms with each other.

If we make the mistake of correcting the older dog for its behaviour to the younger, newer pup, we interfere in the pecking order and big problems can result.

Body language and the new baby

When we bring a new baby into a house where a dog lives, the same procedures as bringing in a new puppy apply. While the dog is away from home for a few hours, drag some of the baby's scented clothing through each room of the house where the dog is allowed to go.

When introducing your dog to your new baby, allow your faithful old friend to come up to you, then give it a big pat. Recognise the dog and then allow it to sniff at the baby's clothing.

Talk to the dog and continue to pat it while holding the baby. Gradually allow the dog to see the new baby and feel relaxed in its presence. The introductions must be done under your supervision — then tell the dog 'Good dog, leave'.

The dog has now made the first contact with this new 'thing'. Remember, to the dog, it's another animal.

Be aware that you should never put the baby down to ground level with the dog, no matter how well trained that dog may be. A dog's teeth and claws can hurt just as much in fun as they can in

Babies put down to a dog's level immediately become subservient. The risk of damage to baby from tooth or claw, even in fun, is high.

anger. Don't put your child at risk under any circumstances. Children's skin cannot take the pawing that another dog's skin covered with thick hair can take.

If you are nursing the baby, don't chastise your dog for wanting to lick the new baby. It will adjust very quickly to this new member of its pack. One lick or close smell will be enough for the dog to identify the newcomer.

Whenever you are nursing the baby and the dog comes up to you, all that is necessary is for you to reach down and pat the dog and possibly give it a 'Down' or 'Stay' command. Remember that, in the dog's mind, it is higher in the pack structure than the baby.

If we understand how the dog sees these and other situations, it is easy to acknowledge the dog and go on with what we were doing.

Never leave a baby and dog together unsupervised — not for one second. Even if the dog has loved children for the last ten years, an accident only takes a second to occur.

Body language and children

It must be emphasised that children and pups or dogs should not be allowed to run around the backyard together. One of the biggest causes of dog bites to children (especially to the face area) is when the dog is allowed to run around the yard when the children are playing.

I know that in all probability you bought the dog for your children. Now you are thinking, 'But she's saying don't let the children play with the dog!' Yes, I'm afraid that is true, especially when the dog is very young.

You see, if you allow the dog to run around the yard with the children, the dog will get used to jumping and running at the children. The dog very quickly thinks that is what children are for. Within a week or two the dog will be biting the children in an attempt to get them to come and play. The dog will not know how to differentiate between the children and another dog. Is this what you want?

Doggy dominance of a child. A child should never put itself in this position.

This is not what you bought the dog for and so, in the first few months especially, you need to keep the dog fairly quiet. All play time must be supervised by an adult who should step in and remove the dog as soon as the jumping and running and chasing start.

Keep your dog out of sight of the children's play, otherwise it will want to play so badly that it will start whining or barking. If you allow your dog to whine or bark, then you are *teaching* it to whine or bark. (You are conditioning it into bad behaviour.)

Put your dog away somewhere out of sight and keep it quiet. You will not have the problems that other people have and the dog will grow into a happy pet with your children.

It is natural for the children to want to play with the new puppy or dog. Parents should teach them how to throw a ball or a squeaky toy or frisby and how to take it from the pup or dog when it brings the toy back. 'Yes! This is what I wanted. Thank you very much.'

Submission

The way in which a dog shows submission to another dog is to go belly to the ground in a drop and then roll over on its back. This exposes the underbelly to the dominant dog, giving it the right to attack and kill if it wishes. Very rarely will a dominant dog do anything to a dog which has reacted in this fashion. The submissive dog has shown, without any doubt, where it is in the pack structure.

The submissive dog, when dealing with a very dominant owner, will assume the same position as above — down, roll over, expose the belly. If the dog is overly submissive, and/or the owner is overly aggressive and dominant, the dog may also urinate at the same time as rolling over. The owner should take a softer approach. The dog's confidence has to be built up. Careful socialising with more people and more puppies may be the way to go.

Total submission by a more submissive dog.

Aggression

An aggressive dog shows the direct opposite to the body language of submission. The arrogant and aggressive dog is completely in control. This dog is afraid of no one, and will use a full display of body language to show to any person or dog just how strong it is.

The truly aggressive dog will raise its hackles, prick its ears up and forward, raise its tail either straight out at the back or arched over the back, pull its lips back to show a full display of teeth, and growl low in the back of the throat.

The aggressive dog has hackles raised, tail up and teeth bared.

This is not a pleasant sight to see. Give this dog a wide berth, if possible. If you own a dog like this, you will need professional guidance and assistance if you are to keep this dog. Normally, such a dog does not make a good family pet. Perhaps you should find another home for it, but it certainly will need very experienced handling.

Fear aggression

On the other hand, the fear-aggressive dog displays a different look. The hackles still rise, the lips may curl back showing the teeth, but the ears normally flatten along the head. The tail either assumes a position out the back or is tucked in between the legs. The eyes quite often have a glazed expression.

Whereas the truly aggressive dog is prepared to stand alone, the fear biter can become very sneaky. This dog is likely to bite when your back is turned, or when you are otherwise engaged and not looking. It will quite often show aggressive tendencies towards other dogs and people, but if the owner walks away, the dog will often back down and follow the owner. The dog very quickly notices that it is not getting the backup it thinks it has. Owners often, inadvertently, encourage fear aggression by their very presence.

Fear aggression is usually caused by something that has happened or not happened early in the dog's life and, unfortunately, it is usually something that a human has or has not done. A hurt caused by mistreatment in some way, or non-socialising of a puppy, can cause this type of aggression. Remember, a puppy is *not* socialised even if it has another, older, dog to play with.

Also, there could be a genetic reason for this fear-timidity. We will cover in chapter 8, 'Puppy management', why socialising with other pups and different-sized people (children) is imperative, particularly when the puppy is between eight and sixteen weeks of age.

As with the aggressive dog, you will require help to overcome this fear aggression problem. Once again, without treatment, this dog does not make a good family pet.

Happy dog

This dog is so easy to read. It will rush to greet its owner with a lick, sometimes jump up (this should not be allowed, however), wag its tail, and even verbalise with a brief, happy bark. Ears sit normally, coat lies perfectly naturally (not raised in a hackle), eyes are very bright and clear — a terrific pet for any family.

The body language of owners

The dog's ability to read our body language is amazing. Your pet can tell:

- when you are not feeling well
- when you are angry (either with it or with someone else in the family)
- when you are tired, frustrated and generally out of sorts
- when you are happy.

Your pet will be able to read you like you are reading this book. It will possibly be aware of your feelings long before any human in your family will know how you are feeling. That's a part of your pooch's natural and wonderful instincts.

Your dog's ability to pick up 'vibes' projected by you or others is unlike ours. We clutter our minds with a thousand and one things which are important to us, but the dog is an *instant and simple* creature. Thousands of years of heritage also play a large part in this area of body language for the dog.

For example, have you ever walked into a room and felt that there has just been an argument between the other people in that room? You get the vibes of anger or frustration that they are emitting. You feel that you should possibly go out and come back at a later time.

Try to multiply that feeling a thousand times. This may give you an idea of how strongly your dog feels the vibes we emit in similar circumstances.

People say 'My dog knows when it has been naughty. I come home, and I see my favourite pot plant has been destroyed while I have been out. The dog cringes as soon as I walk in the gate. It knows it has been naughty!'

No it doesn't!

What your dog is picking up as soon as you notice the pot plant are *your vibes of anger, your different tone of voice and your body language*. These are what is making your dog cringe and back off from you. You are throwing out vibrations of displeasure, and the dog is highly sensitive to this language, because it is the language it speaks.

The dog is reacting to your vibes, your body language and your tone of voice — it does **not** know it has been naughty!

The dog doesn't really know or understand why you are angry. But it is clever enough to read your body language and tone of voice to want to keep out of your way for now.

If you make the terrible mistake at this time of calling your dog, 'Fido, come', and then giving your dog a physical or verbal reprimand, you have now, very effectively, created a problem. Your dog will not want to come near you when you call. Your dog loves you, but it is now confused.

If the punishment you have given your dog at this time is severe, then you will have created a problem which will take some considerable time to correct. Who would want to answer a call to 'Come' if all they receive when they arrive is a severe correction/reprimand? Think about it — you have just arrived home; your dog has waited all day to see you and now it gets roused at!

This is not what you originally set out to do, is it?

All you wanted to do was correct the dog for destroying your favourite pot plant. In the dog's mind, however, he's in trouble for coming when you called, not for destroying the pot plant.

Sorry, but if *you don't catch your dog in the act there is nothing you can do about it.* Hold your anger or frustration and think clearly about what you can do to prevent it happening again.

$\mathcal{C}$ontrol

Reprimands

Sometimes it is necessary to give correction to your pet. Dogs, like children, need direction and teaching. If they deliberately disobey, they need to be made aware that they have done the wrong thing.

Understand, however, that the actions we may consider wrong may have no substance in the dog's mind. For example, the leg of the kitchen chair is not to be chewed. 'But it's made of wood, isn't it, and I can chew any piece of wood I wish when I live in the wild.' To your dog, that's all the chair leg is — a piece of chewable wood.

After all, the dog doesn't sit on the chair and doesn't have to pay for it. What's money to a dog? It is therefore up to us to teach our pet what it can chew and what it can't.

A dog living in a domestic situation has so much to learn. Everything in the house is valuable to humans but of little value to the dog. Nothing is easy for the dog to understand. It is up to you to teach it all it will need to know about living with you. Understanding is important in any relationship. You and your dog need to bond.

When you issue a reprimand to your dog, it is important that you use a method that the dog will associate with getting into trouble.

Instruction and dominance by the handler –
here the pack structure is in order.

Try to emulate its mother as closely as you can. Mum uses her jaws; you can use your hands.

A bitch, when correcting her pup for something it has done wrong, will take the scruff of the pup's neck in her jaws and, depending on the severity of the wrongdoing, will shake the pup, either mildly or more severely. *A bitch is never cruel to her pup, and neither should you be.* Cruelty is to be abhorred, and is *totally* unnecessary.

If your dog is older than a pup, the correction is similar, but instead of taking the dog by the scruff of the neck, you can now grab it by either side of the jowl and, looking into the dog's eyes (eyeballing), shake it and use the word 'No' at the same time.

Children should not be allowed to give this correction. If the dog is dominant and the child is soft-natured, the dog may bite the child on the face. Remember pack structure — you are challenging your dog for the alpha role when you do this.

With a more dominant dog, it may also be necessary for you to put the dog into a dropped position and stand over it. What you are doing in this case is reverting once again to the pack structure. You are the dominant one, not the dog, so you stand over the dog.

Reprimands of any description, however, have to be issued at the correct time for them to be effective. Dogs, being the instant creatures they are, don't think about things for any length of time. Everything to them is *now*.

If two dogs find they don't like each other, the immediate action is to fight. They don't go away and think about the problem. It's instantaneous.

Any reprimand an older dog gives to a younger dog is done immediately. The older dog may growl (watch the younger dog back away) or, if necessary, do more than just growl. If this happens, don't make the mistake of interfering. Leave them alone. They will sort it out. However, if you have a 'bully' in your pack, you will need to be able to recognise the bully and correct it or seek professional guidance.

It is vital that any correction or reprimand we give the dog is at the precise time any misdemeanour occurs. Like the pot plant episode mentioned earlier, you should correct the dog *only* when you catch it in the act. Believe me, your dog will not understand why it's getting into trouble if you correct even just one minute later.

This means, of course, that with a very young dog time has to be spent being patient if you are to catch your pet in the act. You need to watch and learn how your dog thinks, and try to understand why it is doing the things it is doing.

Please don't hit out at your dog with your hands. *Hands are for petting and praising.* Always remember you are working with a dog, *not* a human being.

Body language — a reprimand from
the older dog.

As already mentioned (but I think it important enough to repeat), you will get better and quicker results if you emulate the dog's mother. Hold the pup by the scruff of the neck, or an older dog by the sides of the jowl (face) area.

A *good reprimand* is not a negative action where we are taking out our frustrations on the dog, but is a positive teaching and training process for the new pup or dog.

The five Cs

I have a simple rule of thumb to measure how I am going with the obedience training for my pup or dog:

- Am I *consistent*?
- Am I *constant*?
- Am I *clear*?
- Am I *confident*?
- Do I have *control*?

The first four Cs should give me the fifth — the result everyone wants.

Consistency

Never tell your dog 'No' today but 'Yes' tomorrow. For example, don't allow it to jump up on you and expect it not to jump up on your children. Don't allow it to come into one part of the house today and expect it to stay out tomorrow. Be fair to your pet.

Constancy

Training is ongoing. It remains for you to be constant in everything you do for the rest of your dog's life, be it twelve years or more.

Clarity

Make sure your commands are clear and properly understood by the dog.

Confidence

You must always maintain confidence in yourself and your dog. Know that what you are doing is right for both of you. Without confidence, you will never have a happy home.

Control

If you have all four of the above, you now have the fifth C. What a great relationship you have established with your canine friend!

Praise

As with the reprimands, *praise* must also be given instantaneously. If your dog does something well, praise it — 'Good dog!' Use a very light voice when praising. Put a loving lilt in it. (We'll talk more about voice control shortly.)

Praise is just as important as the reprimand. Always offer praise when it is earnt.

With a very young pup, you will feel that you are doing nothing else but reprimanding, then praising. This is okay, as long as you are remembering to praise. A nice tickle under the chin and a 'Good dog' is usually enough. Don't go overboard with words and hands-on, especially if you have a very active, excitable dog.

Sometimes it pays just to use your voice and keep your hands off. With a very excitable dog, putting your hands on the dog will cause it to become even more excited, thereby causing you additional jumping up or nipping problems. Learn to read your dog's behaviour, and work with the dog accordingly.

However, some form of praise *must* be given for work well done, for doing as you have asked, and for being a good dog. Lack of praise and enthusiasm by some handlers results in a very lethargic and uninterested dog.

It is not contradictory for you to offer praise immediately after giving a reprimand. For example, the pup is caught in the act of chewing your shoe. You have reprimanded it by scruffing its neck, and told it 'Bad dog'. Now you can immediately tell it to 'Sit', and as soon as it does you can praise it. The dog will understand it is getting rewarded (praised) for the sit. A quick tickle under the chin can be enough.

It has now forgotten about the reprimand for the chewing of the shoe even though that was just a few seconds earlier. It will not think it is being praised for destroying your shoe.

(a)

(b)

The 'bad dog — good dog' routine:
(a) reprimand by scruffing the neck;
(b) praise for sitting when told.

What you are doing, effectively, is what is known throughout the dog obedience world as the

'Bad dog — good dog' routine.

It is very effective. *Use it.*

Voice control

Your voice is the best teaching and training aid you have. Learn to use it effectively. Good trainers and instructors will tell you that your voice is 'your lead of the future'.

Because I believe your dog hears the echo your words make, it is very important that you learn to use your voice correctly.

There are three tones of voice to be used for the training of your dog:

- *Command voice*
  When giving your dog a command, use a commanding tone. Don't *ask* your dog to do what you want — *tell* it. For example, 'Sit' is said firmly in a reasonably strong voice, not a quiet, ineffective tone which the dog can either choose to take notice of or very conveniently put in its selective hearing box and ignore.

- *Reprimand or discipline voice*
  When you need to reprimand the dog, *growl* at it if you can — 'Bad dog'; 'Bad chewing'; 'Uh-uh'; 'No'. Words like these *don't* need to be shouted at the dog, but they *do* need to be expressed with simulated crossness. However, *do not* reprimand your dog when you are angry. If you do, you may confuse it and much good work towards obedience will be undone.

- *Happy and joyful voice*
  The third tone of voice is, of course, the light, breezy, happy tone of praise — 'Good dog'; 'Well done'; 'What a great dog you are'.

Learn to use all three tones of voice if you want exceptional results with your obedient dog.

$\mathcal{A}$ nthropomorphism

What a large word — anthropomorphism. What does it mean? According to the dictionary it means 'the ascription of human form or characteristics to a deity or to any being or thing not human'.

To put this into simple terms, anthropomorphism is trying to humanise our pet, or turn it into a little human being. After all, we adopted this little pup into our family, didn't we, so why not make the pup into the child we possibly never had?

It is the humanising of a dog which causes many of the problems we have with our canine friends.

Only about 1 per cent of dogs are born genetically unsound, and yet we continue to have dogs which can cause unending trouble. As discussed in the chapter on pack structure, the ladder of life and control sometimes get out of kilter. It has been found many times that when this has happened it's because the owner has given the dog human characteristics and expects it to live up to the imposed expectations. The owner has *anthropomorphised* it.

Here are two examples.

1. A man owned a six-month-old pup which hopped up on the lounge after playing outside. The dog had not considered that it had been raining. What did it matter to the pup,

Anthropomorphism — cruel expectations
of a non-human creature.

anyway? The owner pushed it off the lounge, threw it a
towel and told it, 'Wipe your feet before you get back on
the lounge.'

Poor pup looked most bedraggled and confused. After all,
that lounge was its bed, and it had been sleeping in the same
spot ever since it had come to live there.

2. A woman with a two-year-old poodle brought home a new pup. She foisted the new addition onto the resident poodle's bed, and when the older dog snapped at the pup, she yelled at the two-year-old and slapped it, telling it 'You're a naughty boy — you should learn to love the darling little puppy, as he's your new brother.'

   Later, the woman expected the older dog to share not only its bed but also its dinner plate. Poor two-year-old and poor puppy. The pup is certainly going to get some beatings from its 'older brother'!

Examples like this show a combination of a lack of understanding of pack structure and the hideous results of anthropomorphising your dog.

How many times have you heard people refer to their dog as 'my darling', 'my little one', 'my pretty baby'? A dog responds to a mind picture and given stimuli (such as body language, tone of voice and noises such as whistles). We use words that dogs have no way of understanding, and when they respond in some way we assume the dog understands exactly what we were talking about. Some owners then tend to anthropomorphise their dog further and further until they smother their pet.

Remember that your dog is a separate species. It doesn't think like you, talk like you, walk like you, eat like you, or indeed do anything else like you. *The dog is not and never will be a human being.* It's only when the dog is allowed to forget its place in the pack that problems arise.

Love your new friend, by all means. That's a perfectly natural, human emotion or feeling. Expect your friend to have *respect* for you as the alpha dog, but don't expect love as we know it in return. Dogs don't love like we do. Some people may like to think they do but, I'm sorry, they just don't.

Love, jealousy, tantrums, wanting to pay you back for something you've done, reprisals, and all the other human emotions (some of which we would be better off without!) should not be thought of as having any place in a dog's character. Your dog operates as an instant creature and doesn't have our hang-ups.

Leave your dog to be what it was born to be — uncomplicated. *Don't anthropomorphise your dog.*

$\mathcal{H}$ealth

Feeding

Here are a few hints and suggestions on feeding your dog.

Some of the food we humans eat is good, healthy food for our dogs. To vary your dog's diet, you may like to add from time to time food such as vegetables (yellow and green), rice, gravy and leftover pieces of meat.

The processed dog foods available give us a tremendous range to choose from. The food companies spend large sums of money to research the basic requirements for our animals. The food is scientifically balanced to give the correct quantities of nutrients, vitamins and minerals required to keep our pets healthy and fit.

Processed foods in tins, or dried, are so convenient. If you are travelling with your pet, you don't have any worries about what you are going to feed it.

On the market at present there are foods specially balanced for the overweight dog, the 'senior citizen', the puppy, and even for dogs with digestive problems.

The dog living in the domestic environment in this country is extremely well catered for. No longer does it have to hunt for a feed. It is all provided for by its human alpha.

There is a tremendous range of good dog
foods to choose from these days.

If you have had your pooch castrated or spayed (desexed), remember to cut back on its daily food supply by about 10 per cent. This, along with plenty of exercise, should keep your dog's weight at a good level. It is always harder to take off weight than it is to put it on.

Many people like to give their dog a bone occasionally. (One a week is fine.) The dog absolutely loves it and it helps to keep its teeth clean. If you feed your dog bones regularly, then watch its weight carefully. If you like to give your dog bones, cut down on the amount of food you put in its bowl. Watch your dog's weight and cut food accordingly.

Here are a few hints about feeding your dog:

- Weigh your dog on the veterinarian's scales regularly.
- Always feed your dog uncooked bones, *never* cooked ones.
- If necessary, reduce the amount of food you give your dog to keep it healthy.
- Check with your veterinarian on when to start giving your growing puppy a bone and for further information on food and weight for a healthy dog.

Worming (intestinal)

Dogs need to be kept worm-free. Worms in dogs can cause many problems to the dog itself and occasionally to the human members of the family. There are several good products on the market; it is simply a matter of choice. Your older dog needs to be wormed at least every three months — more regularly if you and your dog are mixing with a lot of other dogs. Don't forget that when you worm your dog you could also worm the human members of your family. Puppies need to be wormed more regularly until they are at least four months old. Check with your veterinarian for accurate dosage and further details.

Make sure you get into good worming habits with your pet.

Heartworm

If you live in an area where heartworm is prevalent, there are several different ways and methods of giving your pet the heartworm treatment it requires. There is no excuse for not providing this treatment for your pet.

It is extremely important that your pet receives constant treatment for this nasty parasite. It can and will, in time, kill dogs that have not been treated.

Always check with your veterinarian before starting any heartworm program. If your dog has not been on a method of treatment before, it will need to be checked by a veterinarian to ensure that heartworm does not already exist. The veterinarian can diagnose whether or not there is a problem and recommend treatment.

Veterinary care

Make sure that when you take on a dog you have your new friend medically checked immediately. The veterinarian will give you an up-to-date report on its health.

This will give you accurate information on all types of worming and health procedures and put your mind at rest as to what you are to do. If there is some sort of problem, and it is diagnosed early, not only will the problem be minimised but also your pet's full health will be restored faster. You will be saved greater expense further down the track and your dog will enjoy a healthier and happier life.

Dogs, like humans, need regular check-ups. If these are done, possibly on your annual visit to have your dog's parvovirus inoculation, then you will be able to maintain your dog's health at a very high level.

Don't hesitate to contact your veterinarian if you are in doubt about any part of your dog's health and well-being. The vet will be able to help you with the latest development in products you require, and will encourage you to seek obedience trainers/behaviourists who can help you with the understanding and training of your dog.

The den

Dogs need a place to call their own. They require their own space. A dog needs a bed of its own, and an area in which it can relax if it is to remain a happy, carefree pet.

Dogs should have their own beds, and not use yours.

A dog requires something on which to sleep, and there are several very good beds available for your dog. The trampoline type is very good, as it keeps the dog up off the floor. These beds are especially good for the older pet.

Always make sure that your pet has somewhere it can call its own. Ensure that the area chosen is protected from all types of weather. Make sure plenty of fresh water is always available for your dog. (Whether your dog sleeps inside or outside, don't allow it to sleep on concrete.)

Grooming

All dogs need to be kept groomed. Just because they don't have a long coat does not mean that they don't require brushing each day. Even the short- and smooth-coated dogs need to be kept free of loose hair.

A five-minute brush daily will work wonders for both you and your dog — you, because you won't have so many hairs to vacuum, and your dog because it won't be wearing loose hair which can become similar to wearing a fur coat in the middle of summer.

Bathing the dog is all-important, and a good dog shampoo/conditioner should be used. If your dog has long hair, use a good pH-balanced conditioner to prevent its hair from tangling. Leave it on for a few minutes and then rinse it off.

A clean dog is a healthy, happy dog.

Fleas and ticks

There are many different products on the market for these parasites. Seek your veterinarian's advice. Once you have found a suitable product for your pet, stay with it.

With fleas, however, remember that they multiply very quickly (particularly in hot climates) and it is not enough just to treat the dog. The dog's bedding and surroundings should be treated at the same time if you are to successfully eradicate this little monster.

The dog's bedding should be washed regularly and put out in the sun for some hours at a time to keep it fresh.

If your dog spends time inside your home, your home will need to be treated for fleas at least twice a year. I have always recommended 'flea bombs' (with at least a nine-month guarantee period), which you can pick up from your veterinarian. The big advantage of these flea bombs is that they prevent the eggs from hatching. Every flea lays hundreds of eggs and just bathing your dog regularly is not enough. You will be constantly pestered by this problem unless you eradicate fleas from the dog, bedding, surrounds and home.

Dogs also need to be bathed regularly in one of the tick treatment products if a tick problem is prevalent in your area. Should your dog get a tick, it may be necessary for you to take it to your veterinarian for removal. If in any doubt, don't waste time. Ticks can cause paralysis in dogs, and death if left untreated.

$\mathcal{B}$ehaviour

Temperament versus disposition

The words 'temperament' and 'disposition' are often misunderstood when referring to the dog.

Temperament should be used to describe the dog's breeding. For example, a German shepherd of *sound temperament* should be strong, arrogant, slightly aloof with strangers, and very loyal to its owner. Being a herding breed, it is a good worker. It should be confident and follow the owner's lead willingly and immediately. It should be calm under all circumstances, and show its self-assurance.

Its *disposition*, however, is formed by the environment in which it lives and the people it comes in contact with. If it is aggressive, it could be because it lives with aggressive people, or it has been knocked about by the humans who own it, or it has been allowed to act aggressively. This animal now has an unacceptable *disposition*, and yet its *temperament* could be very acceptable.

If a very submissive German shepherd went into hiding every time someone came near it, then it could be said that the temperament of that animal was unsound. This same animal could still be a very acceptable pet in the family and the family may be very happy with its behaviour. So its *temperament* is faulty but its *disposition* is fine.

Be careful that you do not confuse 'temperament' and 'disposition' when trying to decide how to correct a problem or assess the dog's potential.

Only a very small percentage of dogs are born genetically unsound. I am sure you understand that many of the problems we have with dogs are caused by us. We human beings are so often irrational when dealing with our canine companions. We have rarely taken the time to *learn* what makes the canine species tick.

The subject of behavioural problems is very extensive, and many books have already been written to help us understand the causes of some. The following areas are the most common for the average pet owner.

The barking dog

A dog which barks whenever the owner leaves the house is not only a nuisance to the owner, but very annoying to neighbours.

A dog will bark for several reasons:

- it is bored
- it is stressed
- it has got into the *habit* of barking.

Boredom

A dog, particularly one of the working breeds, needs not only physical but also mental stimulation.

I strongly suggest that you take your dog to your local dog obedience club or trainer for basic obedience training. Many things happen when you take your dog for training. The pack structure, with you as the leader, should be strengthened during training. Also, the dog will receive some healthy exercise and some very important socialising.

At the same time, good trainers and instructors will give you a number of suggestions on how to divert your dog's attention from barking. One of the quickest ways, they will tell you, is to move your dog immediately to a quieter location where it can't see whatever it was barking at.

If you never allow your dog to bark more than once, then you are on the way to stopping serious problems from developing.

A continually barking dog becomes the neighbourhood pest.

Stress

People don't realise that a dog can be stressed, especially when it is left alone. If this is happening to your pet, then I will explain one method which may alleviate the problem.

Dogs usually are stressed because they are not totally secure within the canine–human relationship. In other words, they do not feel fully secure when left alone.

'Are you going to come back? Why have you left me? I don't want to be here by myself! I'm lonely because you are my pack and I must have a pack to live with! Without a pack, I am lost and totally fearful (even more so when I am so young).'

These may be some of the fears your pet is experiencing. Remember, you are its pack, its family.

Your dog must learn to trust you, to trust that you will come back, in order to remove the stress.

It is up to you to establish the security your dog needs, and the way to do this is to work on establishing a place within your home in which your dog can feel totally secure. Then work towards maintaining the feeling of security, even though you are not physically there.

I would suggest that during the day when you are at home (or week-ends if that's the only time you are available), put your dog in the area you have chosen. Tether your dog on a two-metre lead and tell it 'Good dog'. (You may like to tether your dog close to where you will be spending some time.) Remember, enforced obedience, when done caringly, is still obedience and leads to good results.

A secure place for your dog will ensure it is not stressed when left alone.

Make sure that there is a small bowl of water handy, and any toys your dog may like to have with it, including a chewable imitation bone. Make this a happy place to be. If you do this right from when it is a puppy, you won't have any problems.

At first, just leave for a short time, possibly thirty minutes to one hour. Go about your normal household chores, and then release the dog from the lead, and have a small game. Do this a couple of times each day, and gradually build up the time the dog is left in this spot.

Your dog will build up a secure feeling when left on lead in this chosen spot.

It wouldn't hurt to tether your dog in this special place at night to sleep. The quicker you make this spot special to your dog, the easier the whole process of anti-stressing will be.

By building up the time the dog is in that place you will be able to leave it secure and comfortable when you go out.

As a further aid to avoiding stress, change your pattern of leaving home. Pick up the car keys earlier and put them in your handbag or pocket. Tether the dog a few minutes before you are ready to leave. Say nothing to the dog. Quietly walk out the back door. Do things in a different pattern from what you have been doing previously.

Remember, if the dog is secure and confident in this special place, you shouldn't have any more incessant barking. It's up to you to persevere. Good luck — it *does* work.

Barking as a habit

Habit barking is harder to cure. Why have you, as the owner and leader, allowed this bad habit to develop?

If you never allow your young pup to bark at people or dogs walking past your premises or the children who are playing next door, you should never have this problem. Teach your pup from the time it comes home that barking is *not allowed.*

The only time you should allow your dog to bark is if someone comes into your yard. Then praise it for giving voice. Use the 'Bad dog — good dog' method:

- 'Bad dog' + scruff the neck for any indiscriminate barking
- 'Good dog' + praise when someone enters your premises.

Dogs actually *learn* to bark. After all, dogs in the wild don't bark all day and not at all at night. If they did, they would soon advertise to all and sundry, friend and foe, where they were, and that would not be wise or desirable.

To stop barking requires patience and consistency from you. Each time the dog barks, you must correct it on the first bark. 'No — bad dog.' This must be on the first bark, because if the dog has already been barking for several minutes, and then you correct it, it doesn't know why it is getting into trouble. A good quick way to stop barking is to remove your dog from the barking situation and place it in another part of the house or yard. Remember, you are the boss, aren't you? So move your dog if you want to.

This will take time and patience. Persevere for results. You will win.

Seek further advice if the problem persists.

Why do dogs like to bark at the postman, for instance? Think about it from the dog's point of view:

postman comes — dog barks — postman goes.

Next day, same thing:

postman comes — dog barks — postman goes.

The dog, with its clock inside it, waits for this daily interruption to its sleepy life. In the dog's mind, when it barks and the postman leaves, the dog has successfully frightened the postman away.

'Aren't I a clever pooch! Look how big and tough I am!'

If the barking at the postman continues long enough, the dog will turn what started out as fun into aggressive barking. By not stopping your dog when it first starts to bark, you may condemn your dog to a life of misery. Your dog is not happy when it is barking and can inherit the unmerited title of 'aggressive dog'. Your once-friendly pup is now considered a pest.

You have the power to turn these negative situations into positive ones. If you can gain the cooperation of your 'postie', give

Habit barking — this must be
controlled at all costs.

him or her a small piece of tasty food to give to your dog. Very soon the dog will look forward to the postman's visit. A negative situation has been turned into a positive one.

Alternatively, when the postman comes, put your dog on a lead, say 'Good morning' and walk away without any barking. The postman leaves and the dog has not, in its mind, frightened the postman away. The dog's aggressive behaviour towards the postman has been reduced because of your control over the situation.

But do not allow any more barking. If necessary, take the dog around the back, out of sight, and give it something interesting to do. Dogs refocus very quickly if you change the location and attitude. This is one of the secrets of successful training.

Digging holes

This is a common problem that should never be allowed to develop. Boredom is one of the causes of hole-digging.

However, hole-digging also stems from your dog's heritage and instincts. Dogs in the wild will sometimes bury parts of their kill to keep it for a future meal. Bitches will scrape away the leaves and undergrowth and make a comfortable hole to bring their litters into the world.

Some breeds of dogs like to get into the earth on very hot days. It's much cooler for them. Sometimes, some breeds just scratch away at the earth and, as the dirt flies around them, it becomes fun.

Scratching and digging — enjoyable for the dog, but a cause of consternation for humans.

Dominant dogs will scratch at the ground after they have been to the toilet. This is not to cover up the droppings, but to distribute the scent as far and as wide as possible.

For whatever reason your dog digs great whopping holes, it is quite frustrating to us as human beings. After all, we've spent some considerable time making that yard and garden a pleasant place to be.

One method of curing hole-digging is to fill up the hole with dog droppings. This will often work, but beware, your dog may stop digging in that spot and find somewhere else to dig.

Another method is to blow up small balloons and place two or three in the hole. Cover with a light layer of dirt, and hope that when your dog next digs, the balloons will be caught by a paw and go off with a bang, giving the dog a fright. What you are doing, in fact, is making the hole *correct* the dog.

Some people have had success by sprinkling pepper in and around the area. If you can think of other ingenious ways to stop your dog digging, use your imagination and try them out.

Chewing

This is a frustrating and annoying habit. Wise owners will work on controlling this habit early in the dog's life.

Catching the dog in the *act* of chewing is the only opportunity you will have to discipline your dog in an attempt to solve the problem. Sometimes, it is better to move out of the way those articles that will be attractive to your dog.

Shoes are a big attraction, especially to pups. They are ideal for chewing on and cutting new teeth. They also contain the human scent of a pack member. 'What a lovely family I have to provide me with such a chewable bone as this!'

Of course, if you give your dog an old shoe to chew, then please

71

don't chastise your dog if it finds one of your very expensive shoes and destroys it. The dog does not know the difference. Just understand it and remove the temptation.

The pup and young dog have a big need to chew. They need to chew on something firm but not too hard. New teeth need exercising, gums need massaging and muscles need strengthing.

As part of puppy training, owners are taught the importance of massaging the puppy's gums and touching the puppy all over its body each day. This therapy has many advantages. It prevents the future problems of owners being frightened of their own dogs. The pup gets used to being handled and fear of other people is removed. This simple procedure eradicates many future problems from the world of dogs.

Touching the pup's mouth each day can help prevent or cure an incessant chewing problem. Put your finger in the side of the pup's mouth and gently massage the gums.

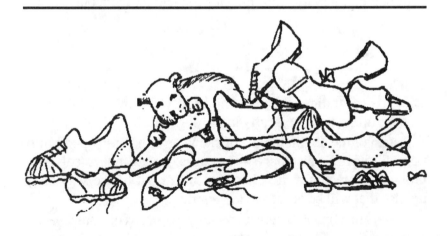

Chewing — a pup must exercise its teeth and gums, so remove temptation out of harm's way.

If your pup is not used to this, you can expect some resistance. The animal may squirm and wriggle and try to get away. Pay no attention to the pup's attitude and start by rubbing the sides of the gums. Do this small exercise several times a day, and see the results it will bring. Pups who will allow you to put your fingers in their mouths tend to become well-adjusted dogs who cease to want to chew everything they come in contact with.

As part of puppy training, owners should touch every part of their puppy's body each day. You should open and examine the puppy's mouth, put your hands in its mouth, feel between the paws of both front and back legs, and examine its ears. When these pups grow up they are never afraid to be handled. (If you are afraid to touch your dog's mouth or any part of it, then a problem is developing or already exists and you should seek help.)

Don't ignore problems, because they only get worse, and remember that in any situation where the dog controls your behaviour, you are *not* 'the boss'.

Chewing, like most bad habits dogs develop, becomes a problem because we allow it not only to develop, but also to continue without any form of correction.

Remember, you have to *teach* what is permissible and what is not. The dog is trying to learn how to live in our domestic situation; it is trying to learn how to live with you.

You are doing your pup, your family, your neighbourhood and your local council a great favour by touching your pup all over each day, especially around and in the mouth. Dogs who have been well handled in this area very rarely become biting dogs or destructive chewers.

But it can't be as simple as that, can it?

Good news!

Yes, it is!

Marking territory — leg cocking

Once again, we are dealing with what to us is a problem, but what to the dog is a very natural part of heritage and instinct.

Understanding that the dog is doing something that comes naturally to it will help you to handle the situation without resorting to anger.

A dog will lift its leg dozens of times in a fairly short distance. What it is doing (and it is mainly the male that does this), is advertising to every other dog which has been this way that it is the biggest and strongest dog around.

Your dog is leaving a calling card. It's a fabulous way dogs have of saying, 'I've been here, and I am now claiming this area as my own. Keep out. Enter if you dare. This is my territory.'

The footpath outside your front gate is *not* your dog's territory. The only area it should be allowed to call its own is inside your gate — your yard.

When walking your dog, don't allow it to lift its leg or, in the case of a bitch, squat. A dog doesn't need to go to the toilet every few metres. With your dog on lead, of course (after all, you are outside your gate), keep your dog walking. If it attempts to squat or lift its leg, tell it 'No' or 'Leave' and keep it walking. Your dog will learn very quickly that it must keep walking at your side when you walk. This will stop your dog from marking territory it does not own.

People have been allowing their dogs to urinate on every tree, lamp-post or building they came to for many years, wrongly assuming that their dog *needed* to do this. No, it didn't. The dog has taken charge of the walk and you are not the boss.

Marking territory is a powerful form of dominance. Watch your dog pee over the spot in your yard that a visiting dog has urinated on. Your dog is saying, 'I'm boss here, not you. Don't try marking

Who's the boss on your walks? Don't let your
dog do this to you.

territory in my domain. I will not allow it.' Hence, it will urinate
over the top.

Some very dominant dogs will even try marking territory inside
the home. Once again, it is trying to tell you that it is in charge.
Don't allow this. Your pack structure has fallen down somewhat,
or your dog would not do this to you.

Realise that, by urinating inside your home, your dog is offering
up a challenge to you as the leader. Accept the challenge. Don't
ever allow your dog to get away with this. Have a look at where
and how you have lost the control you used to have over your pet.
Work quickly on regaining that control.

Using inside the house as a toilet

Sometimes a dog will turn the inside of the house into a toilet after it has been house-trained for months. Experience of handling dog problems for many years has shown that this can be caused by the owner who has allowed the dog to spend far too much time in the house.

The offending dogs are usually small breeds that sleep in the house, are fed inside, are picked up a lot, and stay in sight of the owner day and night. They have forgotten there is an outside.

The solution, of course, is to get the dog outside more often. Keep it outside for as long as possible. Remember, *you are the boss*. Your dog won't like it and may whinge and whine. Persevere — a little each day, and you will cure the problem.

I have dealt with only a few behavioural problems here, the ones I feel are the most common. There are several good books available which deal specifically with behavioural problems. Please purchase one or more of these, and keep them handy (see the reading list at the back of this book).

Always remember that problems are problems only in our minds, never in the dog's mind. The dog doesn't have any hangups. We create the problem, then it escalates, and then when it's finally out of hand we complain about the dog.

Seek professional help before any problem you have with your dog escalates to a dimension that it becomes almost impossible to cure or, at best, will take some months to overcome.

Remember, every vicious, wild, biting dog was (not so long ago) a happy puppy. If the owner had understood and adopted the position of being the boss because the dog needed it, then the dog would still be a happy member of the family.

If bad habits are not allowed to form, there will be no serious problems to cure. Dogs are creatures of habit and conditioning.

Make all their habits good ones, right from when they are puppies. Do not put up with any habit or behaviour that you do not want to continue for the rest of the dog's life. Ensure that all conditioning and teaching you give your dog is constructive.

We have now covered what I feel are the most vital and pertinent points about understanding the dog. Now I will cover some extra features about the puppy.

No manners — the dog has taken over, so the pack structure is out of kilter.

$\mathcal{P}$uppy management

The new puppy owner needs to know and understand certain things about the puppy that has just come into the home. If you have read about and understood pack structure and body language, then directing your puppy into a happy future will be a breeze.

The best time to purchase your puppy from a reputable breeder is at the start of the eighth week — *no earlier, please.*

The five crucial development periods

The pup goes through five crucial development periods from birth to sixteen weeks of age.

The eighth week is the start of the fourth crucial period, and it is extremely important that the pup is not removed from its litter mates before the end of the seventh week. If your pup is to become the socially accepted friend you wish it to be, then it needs that specific playtime — 5 to 7 weeks of age — with its brothers and sisters.

The first three crucial periods occur while the pup is still in the care of the breeder. So the breeder plays an important part in the future disposition of your dog.

A pup who has had a great beginning in life is much easier for you to mould into a happy member of your family.

The first crucial development period

The first crucial period is from birth to twenty days. This is the time when a pup needs warmth, mother, sleep and food.

It requires only a small amount of handling by humans. Perhaps the pup can be just turned over occasionally by the breeder. The pup's mental capacity at this time is very small, almost zero, and its trainability is nil.

The second crucial development period

The second crucial period is from twenty-one days to twenty-eight days (fourth week). This is when the pup still needs warmth, mother, sleep and food, but now all the pup's senses are functioning, and it is aware of life.

This is an extremely important period. *Do not* remove the pup from its litter mates or its mother. Human contact should be introduced, but this contact should be well controlled and supervised.

The third crucial development period

The third crucial period is from the twenty-ninth day to the forty-ninth day (fifth to seventh week). The pup is now capable of responding to voices and is able to recognise people.

Do not remove it from its litter mates. It requires this socialising with its litter mates and with different people. It learns how to play/fight, and how to adjust its bite through playing with the other puppies in the litter.

This is an extremely important period in the puppy's life. Without this play/fight opportunity with litter mates, the puppy may never learn *how to be a dog*.

Problems can develop later in the dog's life if the pup has never been through this time with its litter mates. The dog may not be able to read the body language of other dogs, and it won't be able to display the right body language in return.

You can finish up with a dog which really doesn't know how to socialise with other pups or dogs. That can be a problem which will need care and understanding later.

Your dog's trainability is now developing, and it is now aware of the difference between canine and human.

The fourth crucial development period

The fourth crucial period is from the fiftieth day to the eighty-fourth day (eighth to twelfth week). Your puppy's brainwaves can now be recorded properly. All the brain is waiting for is information. What you teach your pup from now on will be accepted and held in that brain.

Your pup has reached the age where it can now start to form a permanent bond with its human owner. It is now capable of having gentle discipline and accepting gentle methods of training.

This is an *imprint* period. What is put into the dog's brain now will remain. It is now able to learn respect for the alpha leader and will learn by association. Teach small games of fetching, and certainly begin house-breaking.

This is the correct time for the puppy to be removed from its litter mates.

The puppy needs plenty of love and security at this time, and all socialising with children and older dogs should be done under supervision. If the pup gets hurt during this imprint period, this hurt could mentally remain with the pup for the rest of its life.

Don't let children and the young puppy run around the backyard together. If you do, the pup will quickly learn to bite and jump all over the children. Pups and dogs get excited very quickly and jumping and snapping become 'normal behaviour'.

Puppies at play — the fourth and fifth crucial development periods.

You are to become the pup's mother image. It will transfer all its wants to you, now. This is a big responsibility you have taken on, and owning a puppy is not something to be undertaken lightly.

This is the time to start to expose your puppy to common household noises — vacuum cleaners, washing machines, rattling saucepans, carpet sweepers, and so on. Cars starting up and coming home should also be a part of the learning experience. Do it all gently, a little at a time.

This is also the time to start teaching your pup the simple home manners it will require during the rest of its life. Start teaching quietly the 'Sit', 'Drop' and, above all, 'Come' commands.

What your pup learns and experiences during this fourth crucial period (and the fifth) will form the basis of your dog's adult life.

The fifth crucial development period

The fifth crucial period is the eighty-fifth day to the one-hundred-and-twelfth day (thirteenth to sixteenth week). By now, if you have done everything correctly, you should have a well-adjusted, confident, little friend who is not causing too many hassles. The pup still requires socialising, love, attention and security within the family structure.

Its brain is now fully developed, and it is more than capable of understanding all you show and tell it. *If it is capable of learning bad habits, remember, it is equally capable of learning good ones.*

This is the time when your pup will make attempts at becoming the dominant one. Yes, as young as this! If you remember that the pup's mind is still being influenced by all it sees, hears, and is taught, and providing you remember all you have learnt about pack structure, you will be able to discipline and play with your dog successfully.

Your pup is now developing an attitude towards training, and this attitude can be either positive or negative. It's up to you how you go about this training.

At this stage in your pup's life you are teaching. Teach it firmly, but gently. Teach it all its home manners. Leave nothing out. You do want a great dog, don't you? If you don't want it to go into a particular part of the house, then don't let it right from day one.

Because this is the imprint period, be very careful when choosing your puppy training school. When you are attending a puppy play school with your pup, ask the manager to recommend a suitable trainer or club you can contact to carry on your adult training program.

I can't emphasise strongly enough how important it is for you to carry on training with an adult dog training program. Nor can I emphasise enough that you be very selective of your trainer or dog obedience training club. Ask about their training program and

A positive attitude to training — teach your pup firmly but kindly, and you'll have a super dog!

satisfy yourself that they are nice people with a caring attitude and the knowledge you require.

After all, you would choose very carefully the people who will teach your child. So do the same for this adopted member of your family.

Make sure *you* take your dog for its training. You need to supervise all that is happening. Besides, the dog loves you and wants to be with you.

A good training program will give you the encouragement, advice, motivation, and expertise you will need to have the best-behaved and happiest dog in the district.

A bad training program given by an uncaring trainer will only undo all the good you have achieved up to this point.

What your pup learns between the ages of 8 and 16 weeks of age is of vital importance.

This is the most important time of influence in a dog's life. This is when the foundations are laid for a wonderful family friend and a well-adjusted, happy, confident dog. The pup which is traumatised during this time by either another dog or a human can remain antisocial all of its life.

Your pup will become what you allow it to become. Two puppies taken from the same litter and placed in different homes will become dogs with different dispositions (i.e. outlooks, attitudes and behaviour patterns).

The pup learns from its owner what is acceptable behaviour and what is not. The canine–human interaction sets its pattern during this time. If you understand the five crucial development periods, and combine this with what you have learnt about pack structure and body language, you will have *a super dog*!

Helping puppy settle

Congratulations! You have chosen your new companion, and you are ready to take it home. Take a driver with you if you are travelling by car, so you can nurse your puppy while you are in transit. There are two reasons for this: (a) it will help your puppy to get used to travelling in a car and prevent the problem of car sickness arising, and (b) your body will give the puppy the security it needs at this very important time in its young life, thereby starting the bonding process. Remember, you have just separated the pup from its litter mates and, being a pack animal, the pup will immediately start to bond with you and your whole family.

Make sure you have all the items you require for the puppy at home — a stainless-steel feeding bowl, a stainless-steel bowl for water, the food the breeder has recommended, a soft collar, a light lead and, above all, a crate or cage for sleeping in. If your pup will grow into a big dog, then it is wise to buy strong, heavy feeding and water bowls so that the growing, chewing, playful young dog will not chew them up or tip over the water bowl. It is less expensive to get it right the first time.

If your puppy is to make the adjustment from the pack it has lived with for seven weeks to its new pack (the family) happily and with ease, its first night in your home is all-important. This is a little wolf you have taken on, with all the natural heritage and instincts we have already talked about. The manner in which it is introduced into your family is very important to both it and you.

It is also important that each family member is familiar with the rules within which the new member (the pup) is to live. Be consistent and constant always in your directions to the puppy. Be aware that the puppy needs guidance and direction, especially if it is to make the necessary adjustments to living within a human pack. Nothing in your home is as it is in the wild. A puppy has to be taught to live in a domestic situation, so the first few weeks with its new family are crucial to both it and you. Understand that when it chews the leg of your wooden chair it is only chewing a piece of stick. You have to teach it that to chew that particular item is not acceptable to you.

Denning the pup

I believe that where the puppy sleeps on that first day is the most vital part of homecoming. A crate or cage large enough for the puppy to sleep in is the best method of denning the pup. The crate

85

should have air vents for circulation, and should be transportable. An airline crate or a wire crate is wonderful, and the place to put it is on a mat next to your bed. I know, I can almost hear you saying 'I don't want the puppy in the house, let alone next to the bed!' It was your choice to adopt this little bundle of fur into your family, so why put it outside? To the pup, when you do this, you are ostracising it (putting it away from its pack). This can be extremely stressful — it is not the way of the wild, and can lead to early unacceptable habits which you then have to correct. The bonding all puppy owners want will take much longer for you to achieve if you take the line of thinking that dogs must live outside from day one.

Your pup will sleep soundly
in its own personal den beside your bed.

With the crate next to the bed, and an old shirt or socks of yours inside on top of the blanket or bedding, the chance of your puppy sleeping soundly all night is very high. Should it wake, all you have to do is pat the crate and talk quietly to the pup, and it should go back to sleep without any fuss.

The old shirt or socks (which you have worn and not washed before bringing the pup home) provide the comfort of your scent to the puppy. You are now its adopted mum. If it's a cool night or your room is very light, you can throw a sheet or blanket over the top of the crate. This will help the puppy sleep soundly.

This *den* you have so thoughtfully provided for your pup will make the pup feel very secure and safe. After all, the dog in the wild likes to sleep in a confined area, the smaller the better.

A transportable crate can be used in many ways during the first few months of the puppy's life. It can be taken in the car safely (put the seat-belt around the crate), and when you are busy doing chores around the house with a now-mischievious pup getting under your feet, you can pop it in the crate which can be transported from room to room, giving the puppy your much-needed company and keeping it out of harm's way. If the pup is allowed free run of the house, it will get into mischief and you will be continually saying 'no' to the puppy. You may soon develop a negative attitude towards the pup which the crating or denning could have prevented.

If you have to leave the pup at home for any length of time, it is far safer to leave it in the crate where it now feels secure, rather than letting it run loose in the backyard or in the house.

A big plus to all of this is that pups do not like to soil the area in which they sleep, and this will help with house-training. When you take the pup out of the crate, carry it outside and tell it 'toilet'. You will soon have a pup going to the toilet on command. By the way, if you wish, take it up to that area or corner of the yard where you want it to go and you will save yourself a lot of trouble later.

The crate-den can be transported from room to room, keeping the pup safe while still giving it your company.

Of course, as the pup matures and learns all the rules and becomes an obedient member of the family, you can sleep it wherever you wish and not have any problems.

Toys

A puppy needs toys of its own. Chew toys will help with cutting teeth, and a rubber Kong is a wonderful example. If you put some dried puppy food into the Kong, then a little peanut paste, the pup will spend ages trying to get the food out. This is a great idea if you have to leave the pup in its crate when you go out.

Puppies start cutting second teeth around 4 to 5 months of age. Its head, teeth and gums are all changing shape quickly. It is wise to provide something for it to chew on, especially in its first year of life. If you give your pup an old shoe to chew on, don't then blame it if it chews up your good shoes. Give it only chew toys, *not* the type of thing you wouldn't want it to be chewing later.

Remember — what your pup learns during this imprint critical period is all-important. Teach the puppy to be placid and contented just being around you and the family.

Play

Puppies need to be played with, but the type of games you play set behaviour patterns.

Don't play or allow your children to play tug-of-war games with your pup. If you do, you are teaching your pup, which already is a natural predator, to grab at and bite moving hands. *Never* get down on the ground and wrestle with your pup. If you do, your pup will treat you like it would another canine, and you will get bitten. Teeth and claws hurt just as much in fun as they do in anger.

Throw a small, non-collapsable ball or other such object and encourage your pup to bring it back. This way the pup will self-exercise, and get great enjoyment from playing with you or the children. All children's play with the pup should be supervised.

As we said earlier in this book, take your pup to a reputable puppy management class where the teacher will help you overcome any problems that may arise at this early stage. Follow on with basic obedience training and your pup will be a joy for life.

Enjoy your new companion. Love it completely, but make sure it has respect for you as the alpha immediately it comes home, and maintain that respect always.

Puppy management courses

Puppies turn into juveniles and then adults at a much faster rate than humans mature. Blink and you may have missed a very important part of your dog's learning cycle and life.

I've already discussed the five crucial periods and how important they are to the pup's development and its acceptance as an important member of your family. As the pup now matures, it is time to cement that basis you have already formed.

Reread the sections on the fourth and fifth crucial periods. I will enlarge on them a little more.

The first visit to a course

A normal common fear for first-time owners at a puppy management course is 'Will there be large aggressive pups there who will intimidate my tiny little helpless pup and perhaps hurt it?' The pup, on the other hand, hasn't a clue where its new owner is taking it until it gets there. Then, when it sees the other pups of all sizes and shapes, it thinks 'Holy Moley, what is this place? What are these other creatures? What am I supposed to do with them? My litter mates didn't look like any of these animals, and just take a peep at

'Protect me please'

that massive giant over there. My goodness, he's coming over here. Help!!!!!! Mum, Dad, where are you?'

Yes, nearly every pup that goes to puppy training is worried and insecure as it faces up for the first time. This is normal and occurs regardless of size or breed. A large German shepherd pup can be just as frightened as a small Jack Russell on its first visit. The good trainer will read the pup's body language, point it out to the owner, and allay any fears. Within hours, however, and sometimes even within minutes, the pup will show signs of becoming more confident. It is an amazing sight, and one that a trainer never tires of. The ability of even the smallest and most insecure puppy to cope with and grow through these 'threatening' experiences never ceases to amaze me. You will be amazed that you might not take home the same puppy you brought with you an hour or two earlier. It is true. Your puppy seems to have changed before your very eyes.

Other visits

As the classes progress each week, the puppy could be handled by many different people. This is important, as your pup needs to accept other people and not be afraid. Others may check the puppy's ears and eyes, handle its feet (nails have to be clipped) and handle its mouth (this plays a very important role later on when you may have to remove something from its mouth). The pup who is taught early to allow people to put their fingers in its mouth does not bite fingers when it is older. The pup who is raised unafraid of people during this fourth crucial period (eight to twelve weeks) will very rarely become aggressive towards people as it grows to maturity. Don't make your fingers an intrusion. Make them very acceptable by putting some soothing gel on them and rubbing the gums, or by just being gentle when putting your fingers into the pup's mouth. New teeth are coming through at this time, and the pup's mouth may be sore.

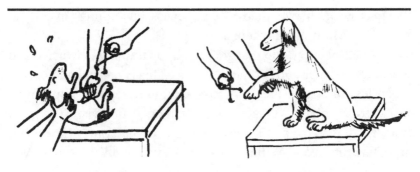

First-time blues   'It's not so bad after all.'

Nail clipping

Dogs' nails need to be clipped regularly to keep them at a correct length. Teach them as a pup by handling their feet and trimming their nails. Don't clip them too short. Just take off the tips — once a week until the pup gets used to it and then once a month should be enough. Teach it when it's young and you will not have any problems as it gets older.

Puppy play

If puppy play and socialising is done under proper supervision, very rarely will the pup have problems with other dogs as it matures. It accepts all sizes and shapes. It is fascinating to watch a group of puppies playing. Watch the body language. You can learn lots about the character of your individual pup. Some are dominant, some submissive, some boisterous, some noisy, some quiet and some may even be a bit of a bully. All of these different characteristics can be displayed at some time or other by most of the puppies during these weeks of socialising. You will find it fascinating to watch the pup who is at first timid, quiet and very submissive change on each subsequent visit and as each week progresses.

The good puppy management trainer constantly observes all the puppies and adjusts the play behaviour where necessary. For example, if a 'bullying' puppy's manner is not recognised and corrected as it occurs, this puppy may be a bully for the rest of its life. This pup needs either a quick, firm correction by the owner or the person in charge of the class, or picking up and putting down in another play area. All this little one needs is to be gently but firmly shown that this behaviour is unnecessary and unacceptable. If the pup with bullying tendencies is not recognised or corrected at this early age, the chances of it becoming an acceptable part of domesticity is made more difficult for the owner. Timing of any correction given is all-important.

The above behaviours are normal and they need to be observed and worked through early. The quiet, shy puppy can change to become an outgoing, social, well-adjusted and well-behaved little being that is a joy to have around. This early socialising and play behaviour modification is one of the reasons puppy training is so very important.

Early teaching versus formal training

Teaching

We are still in the fourth crucial period. Please refer to that section and reread it thoroughly.

Your selected trainer should carefully take you through this very important period. All the basic exercises will be taught at this time, as well as the play sessions.

I repeat words I've used before and will use again — the pup that is taught these basic exercises never forgets them, particularly if they are taught gently but firmly, with love, fun and consideration.

There are many ways to do these exercises, and the different breeds sometimes require different methods, but if everything is taught in a fun and caring manner, the pupply will accept that working for a reward, even if it is just a pat, is normal. *Remember, the dog in the wild has to work for all it gets. Nothing is handed to it.* Food, warmth and companionship all have to be earned and worked for. If it doesn't hunt and kill, it doesn't eat. It is not hard for the puppy with its basic instincts to accept that it has to *give to get.* Just start with a simple 'sit' and then reward with a titbit, and a 'Good pup'. This can be done before each meal, for instance. It can be done with the sit, the down or the stand. Your trainer will show you how to do this.

With your trainer's assistance, at the end of a few weeks your pup should come every time it is called. The pup who comes on the first call every time runs very few risks of getting hurt or into trouble as a full-grown dog. The benefits from just this one exercise have to be seen to be fully appreciated. And remember — reward, *reward*, REWARD.

Training is the word used after the pup has reached 12 weeks of age. Read again about the fifth crucial period. The puppy's concentration is now improving each day, and it is more than capable of absorbing more and more. You can teach it anything you wish, but remember to make it *fun, fun, fun.* Fetching balls, roll overs,

'I love you. I'm coming real fast.'

hand shakes and so on are great little exercises. The pup who is taught to think gets great enjoyment out of life. It learns to look forward to its activities and consequently doesn't get into a lot of mischief.

When owners spend quality time with a pup, great benefits are seen. The bonding that occurs at this time can never be recreated to the same extent should you delay training until your dog is an adult. Your 'alpha position' is now being established, and the pecking order accepted, understood and appreciated by all. Be consistent with all training. You've *shown* the pup how you want it done in the previous crucial period — now is the time to *expect* the pup to carry out the commands you may give.

Read again the section on control and the five Cs (chapter 4).

I'm being very obedient. I can...

sit   down   stand

Be consistent, constant, clear, confident, controlled. I'll even add another — be calm.

$\mathcal{T}$he future

Life after puppy training

When your pup reaches about sixteen weeks of age, it is time to move along. Take it to a reputable trainer (if your current puppy trainer doesn't take them further) who will help you to further stabilise all you and the pup have learnt. The concentration level of the pup has increased even more. It may now be four to six months old and is what I class as a 'juvenile'. This young dog now needs something more substantial to think about.

Go to a trainer who conducts class sessions, as this will further help your dog in the socialising area. If your situation doesn't allow you the time to take your dog to classes, then be even more selective with your trainer. It is not always a good idea to send a dog so young away for training. Just being away from home can be stressful enough and, should the trainer be in any way harsh with the dog, it can leave a fearful impression on the very young dog which can last a lifetime, and all the good work you have already done is in jeopardy.

'Training', like 'teaching', is meant to form a wonderful bond between dog and handler and you and your family can receive great benefits by taking the time to take your dog to classes.

Classes may be thought about like this:

- puppy management classes — kindergarten
- juveniles — primary school
- adult classes — secondary school
- advanced, competition, agility, fly ball, tracking, etc. — university.

Do it all. You'll enjoy it and so will your dog. Training provides mental as well as physical stimulation for both of you. For the great majority of dogs, this training will be sufficient to stop them from being bored. It is when a dog gets bored that it digs holes, plays with the clothes on the line and destroys your garden. Dogs that enjoy regular training rarely cause domestic problems.

On the way to maturity

At different stages of your dog's life, it will go through difficult times. Four to five months (teething time) can be and often is a fear period. Small things may upset the dog. Training at this time can be most helpful as it will build the dog's confidence. Around eight months of age the dog's head is fully developed and the second teeth now settle firmly into the gums. This can cause some pain around the mouth area for a few weeks. Fortunately, most fear periods last for only a short period of time.

Twelve to fifteen months can be another fear period and the dog may need reassurance from its owner. Don't let it get away with anything, though. Understand but don't condone any sign of misbehaviour. At eighteen months the dog is starting to reach maturity (especially in the smaller breeds), and now thinks it is a big macho dog. It may try again and again to take over the pecking order. Firmness at this time is all-important (see chapter 2, 'Pack Structure').

'What is that? Will it hurt me if I touch it?'

The larger breeds such as German shepherds, Rottweilers, Dobermans etc. reach full emotional and mental maturity any time between two and three years of age (this is a fairly general statement), whereas the smaller breeds like terriers reach maturity around fifteen to eighteen months.

As your dog matures, make sure it always reacts to your requests in the desired manner. If it doesn't, don't assume your dog has suddenly got out of control. It has taken some time to get to that state. Think again about the pecking order. There may even be a very good doggy reason. Perhaps a check with the vet would be a good idea. Don't forget, there could be a physical reason for unwarranted behaviour. Always be kind and understanding while being fair, and your pup will love you regardless, even though you are asking for absolute respect.

Other understandings

It is very important that the differences between the small and the large breeds are recognised. If you own a small breed, understand

'Hey! I'm talking to you.
Don't ignore me, big guy!'

that it is only small in size. It is as large in heart, mind and instincts as any large breed. It thinks it is huge and acts accordingly. It may even issue a challenge to a much larger breed (sometimes silently), and then not have the physical ability to handle what it may have started.

Watch when two dogs meet. If there is any sign of fear, one dog may issue a 'calming signal' by turning its head to one side. It is saying to the other dog 'I am not interested in anything you may want to start — just leave me alone.' In the animal world, the stronger, more dominant dog will very rarely hurt the submissive dog. It will, in most instances, respond to the signal immediately. (For more information on 'calming signals', read *On Talking Terms with Dogs: Calming Signals* by Turid Rugaas.)

You can also use the same calming signal to your dog if you wish to defuse a situation. Turn your head to the side and walk away.

This signal is also often given by the dog to young children who are annoying it. Unfortunately, most don't see it for what it is and, if this signal is ignored over a period of time, the dog will react and the child may get bitten. Parents and other adults in the house need to be aware of what is happening when the dog does this to a child, and tell the child to move away.

Training for a dog is for the rest of its life. This doesn't mean you have to continue going to training classes. It does mean that you, as the alpha, never allow the dog to disobey when it is told to do something. For example, if a dog, at nine years of age, does not sit when you tell it, then go over to the dog and firmly put it in the sit position. Watch the next time you tell it to sit. It will probably sit immediately. It's the little things that happen that ensure you have a loyal, obedient dog for the rest of its life.

Investigate 'competition' work for your dog as it matures. It can be fun for you and great fun for your dog. There are many fields in which you and your dog may take part, depending on the breed:

- obedience work for all
- gun dog work and field trials
- agility for most breeds, after eighteen months of age — allow the dog to develop physically before doing these amazing jumps
- tracking, herding, luring and others are very attractive sports.

Have fun with your dog and it will always be the pleasure it was as a young cuddly puppy.

Enjoy your companion for life.

$\mathcal{R}$ating summary

The following short honesty check will tell you 'Who's the boss' in your household.

Please write down your answers to the following questions.

1. If you and the dog arrive at the door together, who walks through the door first?

   You/Dog   *Answer*..............

2. When the dog scratches at the door to be let out or to be let in, do you jump up immediately?

   Yes/No   *Answer*..............

3. Who has dinner first?

    You/Dog   *Answer*............

    (If you wish to establish pack leadership in your home, you and the family should eat first. The dog should be put on a long 'Down', i.e. in a dropped position, some-where nearby. It should be expected to stay quiet for the whole time you are having your meal. Under no circumstances feed your dog from the table. In order to establish authority, make it wait for its meal.)

4. Does the dog take you for a walk, rather than you taking the dog?

    Yes/No   *Answer*............

    (Do you take your dog for a walk at the same time each day? Is your dog ready to go before you are? Or do you decide when and where you will take your dog for a walk? Different times for your dog's walk are recommended, especially if you are trying to establish more control over your dog. Softies always give in when their dog comes up at the appointed time with big eyes which say, 'Aren't you taking me for a walk today?' Just remember, each time you give in to your dog, it takes a little bit of power back. This is fine if you have a friendly, happy, untroublesome pet, but it is *not* fine if you are having any problems with your dog.)

5. Do you walk around your dog if it is lying down?

    Yes/No   *Answer*...........

6. Who is most comfortable on your bed?

   You/Dog   *Answer...........*

   (If you allow your dog to get up on your bed, you run
   the risk of serious pack structure failure. All your good
   training and discipline can be undone by allowing your
   dog to lie on the same level as yourself. Dominant dogs
   will take the ascendancy and will not understand your
   trying to give them an order later on. They will not want
   to obey you because they don't think they should. Training will be harder, longer and more confusing. Putting
   your pup or young dog on a mat at the side of your bed
   for bonding purposes is recommended.)

7. Do you allow your dog to bark whenever it
   feels like it?

   Yes/No   *Answer...........*

   (A trap that many people fall into is allowing their dog
   to bark because they want it to be a 'watch dog'. There
   is no need for this. As a matter of fact, it is extremely
   dangerous to allow this habit to start. The dog will very
   quickly turn an occasional barking situation into many
   barking episodes. Now you have a nasty public nuisance
   in your yard instead of a friendly pet. Don't worry about
   your dog protecting you when the occasion arises. It will
   certainly bark and let you know when someone or
   something comes into the yard. Remember, that is the
   dog's territory. If your dog barks, you should go out
   immediately and check the situation. The dog has no
   right to bark at people going up the street, but can be
   rewarded if it is letting you know that someone is
   coming onto the property.)

8. Do you allow your dog to dig holes in the garden or lawn?

Yes/No   *Answer*.............

9. Does your dog growl at you if you touch its food?

Yes/No   *Answer*.............

(Seek a good trainer immediately if it does. Under no circumstances should your dog growl at you. If it does, then the pack structure is out of order and more social-ising and some advice is necessary.)

10. Does your dog demand you play with it by dropping a ball or stick at your feet?

Yes/No   *Answer*.............

11. Do you always obey your dog's commands?

Yes/No   *Answer*.............

(Softies will always give in to their pet's demand to play. There is nothing wrong with this as long as you are not having any problems with your dog. If you are having any disobedience problems, then don't play with your dog just when it wants it. Take control and you decide when and where to play with the dog.)

12. Does your dog ignore you when you call it?

    Yes/No   *Answer.............*

13. Does your dog run away from you?

    Yes/No   *Answer.............*

14. Does your dog have its own lounge chair, and bite you if you touch it?

    Yes/No   *Answer.............*

    (If it does, seek help immediately. Most family pets will very quickly respond to a good trainer's touch and your problems are quickly solved.)

15. Does your dog create a fuss when you go out and leave it?

    Yes/No   *Answer.............*

16. Does your dog wriggle and squirm when you want to groom it and cut its nails, and look at its ears?

    Yes/No   *Answer.............*

17. Does your dog refuse to eat the dinner you have provided?

Yes/No   *Answer.............*

(Some people get anxious when their dog doesn't eat its meal. They then go chasing after different types of food, and when the dog finds one to its satisfaction, that's the one they say their dog likes. The owner may then fall into the trap of saying, 'My dog won't eat anything but rib fillet.' There are many good foods on the market and any one of them may be very suitable for your dog. Don't let your dog dictate to you what it will eat and what it won't. Mix up its food from time to time; you may add things like vegetables, gravy, rice. Talk to your vet if you need further advice on food and nutrition.)

18. Does your dog suffer from selective hearing?

Yes/No   *Answer.............*

19. Does your dog continually jump up on you and your friends?

Yes/No   *Answer.............*

20. Does your dog ever growl at you when you chastise it?

Yes/No   *Answer.............*

21. Has your adult dog ever lifted its leg in the house after it has been toilet-trained, especially if it is over two years old?

Yes/No   *Answer*.............

If you answered 'Yes' or 'Dog' to any of the above questions, then you and your family have some interesting dog obedience problems to solve. What are you going to do about this?

I believe that if you have read this book thoroughly, and are prepared to adjust your thinking to your dog's way of thinking, then you will know how to go about correcting any misbehaviour or habits that you no longer want.

Good luck and congratulations.

$\mathcal{R}$eading list

Your nearest bookstore or library will have some interesting books about dogs. Include in your reading at least one book about the particular breed of dog you own. Then discuss what you have read with others who have some experience with breeding dogs, obedience training of dogs, or the shaping and direction of dog behaviour.

The following is a very short list of books about dogs. This sample illustrates the diversity of information available about our 'best friend'.

The Monks of New Skete (1991). *The art of raising a puppy.* Boston: Little, Brown.

The Monks of New Skete (1978). *How to be your dog's best friend.* Boston: Little, Brown.

Bruce Fogle (1994). *101 questions your dog would ask its vet.* London: Penguin.

Bruce Fogle (1990). *The dog's mind.* London: Penguin.

J.M. Evans and Kay White (1985). *The doglopaedia (a complete guide to dog care).* Surrey: Henston Ltd.

Ian Dunbar (1979). *Dog behaviour (why dogs do the things they do).* Neptune, NJ: T.F.H. Publications.

Michael W. Fox (1972). *Understanding your dog*. New York: St Martins Press.

John Paul Scott (1958). *Animal behaviour*. Chicago: University of Chicago Press.

Gary Turbak (1987). *Twilight hunters (the wolf)*. Flagstaff: Northland Publishing Co.

David Alderton (1987). *The dog care manual*. London: New Burlington Books.

Carol Lea Benjamin (1981). *Dog problems*. New York: Howell Book House Inc.

William Koehler (1988). *The Koehler method of dog training*. New York: Howell Book House Inc.

American Rescue Dog Association (1991). *Search and rescue dogs (training methods)*. New York: Howell Book House Inc.

Joel M. McMains (1992). *Dog logic: companion obedience (rapport-based training)*. New York: Howell Book House Inc.

Job Michael Evans (1985). *The Evans guide for counseling dog owners*. New York: Howell Book House Inc.

Job Michael Evans (1988). *The Evans guide for civilised city canines*. New York: Howell Book House Inc.

William E. Campbell (1992). *Behaviour problems in dogs*. California: American Verterinary Publications Inc.

David Weston (1990). *Dog training, the gentle method*. Melbourne: Hyland House.

Michael Tucker (1980). *Dog training made easy*. Willoughby: Weldon Publishing.

Ross Allan (1996). *Dog obedience training*. Neptune City, NJ: TFH Publications.

Turid Rugaas (1997). *On talking terms with dogs: calming signals*. Kula, HI.: Legacy By Mail, Inc.

$f$eedback

If you would care to give some feedback on how you viewed this book, then please fax or write to:

Val Bonney
34 Romea Street
THE GAP
QLD   4061
Australia
Fax (07) 3300 9787

Email: bondog@powerup.com.au
Web page: http://www.powerup.com.au/~bondog/

MRS B DRAPER
MEADOW VIEW
RUGBY ROAD
LONG LAWFORD
RUGBY
WARKS CV23 9DN